ENRIQUE'S DAY

Para los niños huamanguinos que fueron mi padre y mi tío Renan,
también para Jesús y Ximena, y los demas niños de Huamanga

First published in Great Britain in 2002 by Frances Lincoln Limited,
4 Torriano Mews, Torriano Avenue, London NW5 2RZ

British Cataloguing in Publication Data available on request

ISBN 0-7112-1933-8

Designed by Sophie Pelham

Printed in Singapore

1 3 5 7 9 8 6 4 2

AUTHOR ACKNOWLEDGEMENTS
Un tremendo abrazo de agradecimento para Antonio Ramos (me diste el aliento para realizar este trabajo), El Centro de la Fotografía,
Javier Zapata y mis colegas del departamento de fotografía, mi familia, James Reynolds, the del Barco School for Young Journalists,
Maricela y Jesús, Dinamita, El Colegio Salesiano, la ciudad de Huamanga, mis ángeles Pati, Sandra, Loreto, Jenne, Carla, Cristy, Susana,
mi querida madre, y, por supuesto, mi editora Cathy Herbert.

A tremendous gratitude-filled hug for Antonio Ramos (your advice and support made this possible), El Centro de la Fotografía,
Javier Zapata and everyone in the CARETAS photography department, my family, James Reynolds, the del Barco School for Young Journalists,
the city of Huamanga, my ever-present angels: Pati, Sandra, Susana, Loreto, Carla, Cristy,
my mother, and Jenne, and of course to my wonderful editor Cathy Herbert.

ENRIQUE'S DAY

From Dawn to Dusk in a Peruvian City

Sara Andrea Fajardo

FRANCES LINCOLN

AUTHOR'S NOTE

Enrique lives in the city of Ayacucho, which is perched on one of the world's tallest mountain ranges, the Andes. Ayacucho is full of city noises and city smells. If you came to visit, you would notice *caseritas* (street traders) on every corner: perhaps someone selling homemade yoghurt or bread, or a medicine made from snakes and herbs. With all the bustling activity, it is very difficult to sleep late. Most people are up and about before the clock strikes six – even before this, the city buses and motor-taxis are honking their way through the streets.

Enrique's favourite day of the week is Sunday, when most of the shops are closed, and Peruvian families get together to spend the day. Enrique especially looks forward to trips to *el campo,* the countryside, where there are outdoor restaurants that serve delicious foods like *cuy* (guinea pig). On days like this Enrique and his family talk about all the things that have happened in the week and Enrique tells them the latest jokes he has heard at school. On the way back home, he and his little sister Ximena do what *Ayacuchanos* (people from Ayacucho) love most – they sing at the top of their voices!

PERU

Ayacucho

SOUTH
AMERICA

Jesús Enrique Fernández is seven years old. His family likes to call him 'Enriquito', which means 'little Enrique'.

Enrique lives high up in the Andes mountains, in the city of Ayacucho, with his parents and his younger sister Ximena. His father, Jesús, manages the family bakery, and his mother, Maricela, runs the family café.

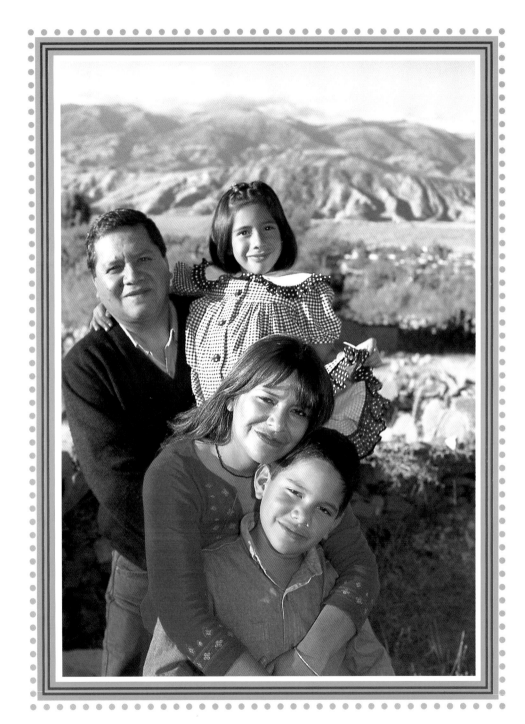

1

Just before the cock crows at half-past six, Enrique is up and ready to start the day. He puts on his school uniform, and his mother helps him comb his hair. Enrique is still yawning as he ties the laces of his shoes, which he polished the night before.

Enrique's first task of the day is to get the *chaplas* from the corner bakery, where the bakers have been busy working since four o'clock. Nothing goes better with chaplas than *Milo*, a chocolate powder which you stir into hot milk. Enrique loves dipping the crispy chaplas into his Milo and making them go all soggy.

CHAPLAS are a type of flat bread, made only in Ayacucho. The ovens used to bake them are usually very old and don't have temperature gauges. The bakers say that they can tell when the oven is hot enough simply by looking at the colour of the fire's flames.

By half-past seven, Enrique and his mother are waiting at the street corner to hail one of the hundreds of motor-taxis that zip through the streets. Enrique's motor-taxi this morning doesn't have a door, so he enjoys feeling the wind on his face as he goes.

No matter what route Enrique takes, he always passes two or three Catholic churches. He can hear the flower and candle sellers calling out to the churchgoers, asking them to buy something for their favourite saint.

Many of the houses and shops that Enrique sees along the way have models of churches, bulls or musicians on their rooftops. These ceramic sculptures are believed to protect the buildings.

Enrique's *escuela* (school) is a colonial building, like many buildings in the city. He runs through the huge colonial archways in a hurry to greet his friends, Quispe, Durand and Arias.

The colonial buildings of Ayacucho date back to the time when Peru was a 'colony' of Spain. Peru finally broke free from Spain and became independent about two hundred years ago, in 1824.

The school day always begins with assembly. All the pupils sing Peru's national anthem and say a prayer together before going into school.

Enrique attends a Catholic school so their prayer is a Catholic one. Most people who live in Ayacucho, and most Peruvians, are Catholic. There are 33 Catholic churches in Ayacucho alone!

Señor Livia, Enrique's teacher, starts by taking the register and checking that everyone has remembered his homework. The first lesson is maths, Enrique's favourite. Enrique would like to be an astronaut when he grows up, but he knows he needs to pass lots of maths exams first.

Enrique and his friends volunteer to go up to the board. Then Señor Livia writes up some equations and they have a race to see who can solve the problems the fastest. As usual, Enrique is the first to finish!

It is soon time for *refrigerio* (snack break). Enrique usually eats chaplas for refrigerio, but today his mum has given him money to buy something from the *kiosko* (tuck shop). He chooses strawberry flavoured gelatine, which tastes delicious in the late morning sun.

Enrique and his friends are drinking Inca Kola, *Peru's most popular soft drink. Peruvians drink Inca Kola with everything. It tastes especially good with their two favourite foods:* cebiche *(fish cooked with lemon) and* chifa *(Chinese food).*

When refrigerio is over, Enrique has a PE (Physical Education) lesson. The school is in the middle of a big basketball tournament, and Enrique is learning some new techniques.

At the end of the morning, *mami* (mum) picks up Enrique and Ximena and they walk to the market. The buildings that they pass are made out of stone and adobe (bricks moulded from mud and straw).

12

There are so many things to see at *el mercado* (the market) that Enrique doesn't know where to look first.

Many of the market sellers are native *Quechua* people, and wear traditional dress. Quechua women from Ayacucho wear square-shaped white hats and full skirts called *polleras*.

QUECHUA is the name of the South American Indian people who live in this part of Peru. You can tell which town or village a Quechua person comes from by the shape and colour of their hat or, if it is a Quechua woman, by the style of her llikllita *(shawl).*

13

The fruit and vegetable section makes Enrique's mouth water. There is much to choose from – even black and purple varieties of potato. Today Enrique's mother is looking for an avocado. Enrique picks one that is soft and ready to eat.

El almuerzo (lunch) is the biggest meal of the day in Peru. As a special treat, Enrique's mother takes them to an outdoor restaurant. Ximena orders *chicharrones* (fried pieces of pork), and Enrique and his mother order their usual, *cuy frito* (fried guinea pig).

CUY Andean Peruvians have eaten guinea pigs for thousands of years, since long before the Inca Empire. Scientists say that it is one of the healthiest meats a person can eat, because it contains lots of protein and very little fat.

When they get home, Enrique's mum takes some oranges and glasses of *chicha morada* (a sweet drink made from purple corn) out into the garden. Then they settle down to read some stories together.

Enrique loves playing *futbolín* (table football). Every time he scores a goal he shouts "G-O-O-O-O-L!!" just like they do during matches on television.

Football is Peru's national sport. Whenever there is an important match, people paint their faces with the colours of their chosen team and, if their team wins, they celebrate by singing in the streets.

At about five o'clock, Enrique's *papi* (dad) takes the children to their favourite place in Ayacucho – Moreno's sweet shop. Ximena is still little so she needs her father to lift her up to reach the lollipops. Enrique chooses chocolate-coated cookies.

Every visit to Moreno's sweet shop is followed by a stroll in the *Plaza de Armas* (town square). Enrique and Ximena run round the statue of *Sucre* and climb the lampposts until papi says it is time to go home.

SUCRE Antonio José de Sucre was the military general who led the Battle of Ayacucho, the battle that freed Peru from Spanish rule.

Later in the evening there is a procession in honour of the patron saint of Enrique's school, *María Auxiliadora*, (Mary, Helper of Christians). Enrique and his school friends have each made a lantern to carry with them as they walk in front of the float.

It takes more than fifty men to carry the float through the streets because it is so heavy. It is made from eucalyptus logs that have been built up into a pyramid, covered with white wax and then decorated with handmade flowers and candles.

The procession lasts for more than two hours. Afterwards Enrique changes out of his school uniform and warms himself up with a cup of *café con leche* (milky coffee) at the family's café. Ximena always thinks Enrique's food looks nicer than her own, so Enrique lets her have a bite of his chicken sandwich.

Before bedtime, Enrique needs some help with his maths homework. His papi goes through each problem with him, and makes sure that Enrique understands by asking him lots of questions.

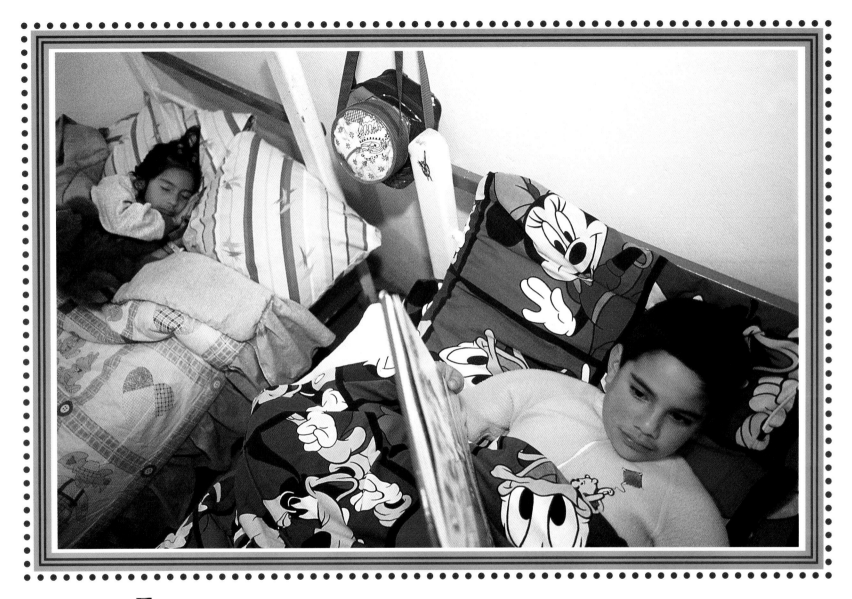

Enrique is very tired after his busy day. He only reads a few lines of his book before whispering, *"Buenas noches, Ximena,"* (Good night, Ximena), and turning off the light.

MORE ABOUT PERU

PERU, THE LAND

If you took a bus across Peru you would pass through jungle, mountains and desert. You would need to be well prepared as the journey wouldn't be easy. High up in the Andes mountains, for example, the air is so thin that some visitors have had to wear oxygen masks just to be able to breathe. The Peruvian jungle offers a very different kind of adventure. Everything that lives there, be it animal, insect or plant, grows to be enormous. Some species of ant are the size of an adult's thumb!

Peru only has two seasons: wet and dry. People are careful not to get caught in the rain during the wet season because the raindrops are so heavy and fall so quickly that you can be drenched in seconds.

PERU, THE PEOPLE

Every village, town and city in Peru has one thing in common: a *Plaza de Armas* (town square), where Peruvians go to see and be seen. Each Plaza has gardens and walkways for people to enjoy, and usually a fountain or a statue right in the centre. Local parades or religious processions always begin and end at the Plaza, and all the most important buildings in the town are built around this central area.

Peruvians have two passions: family and football. Sundays in Peru are set aside especially as a time to spend with the family. Even after people get married, they remain very close to their parents – sometimes people build extensions onto their homes so that they can all carry on living together. One of the things Peruvian families enjoy doing most together is watching football. The whole country seems to come to a standstill when the Peruvian national team plays because everyone stops what they are doing to watch the match!

Despite all the things Peruvians have in common, every town in the country is unique, with its own foods, traditions, music and clothing. Communities that are only separated by a few miles will each offer something different, whether this is a speciality cheese, sweets, or the little wooden boxes filled with carvings of Andean characters, made in Ayacucho.

PERU, THE PAST

Ancient Peru was the birthplace of a series of advanced and brilliant cultures, which eventually came together in the glorious Inca Empire. The people of the Inca Empire worshipped the Sun God, Inti. They built large stone temples in his honour which they decorated with gold. The Inca himself (the Emperor), was believed to be a descendant of Inti, and wore splendid robes encrusted with gold jewellery and precious stones.

So when the Spanish conquistador (adventurer), Francisco Pizarro, and his men arrived in Peru in 1531, they must have felt that they had discovered a golden land. The Inca Empire fell under Spanish rule and Peru became known as the Pearl of the Spanish Empire. It wasn't until 1824 that Peru broke free from Spain and became independent. Peru is now a modern democratic nation, but the ancient ruins you can see wherever you go are a constant reminder of the country's rich and interesting past.

RELIGION IN PERU

Most Peruvians are Roman Catholic – the religion that was brought to Peru by the Spanish. However, Peruvians are still heavily influenced by the beliefs of their ancient ancestors. They often talk about the Earth goddess, *Pacha Mama*, and it is traditional in the Andes to pour a bit of your drink on the ground as an offering to the Earth.

LANGUAGE IN PERU

Most Peruvians speak Spanish, the language of Peruvian television, newspapers, books and politics, but many other languages are spoken around the country. Of these, Quechua is the most widespread. The people of Ayacucho are nearly all bilingual – they speak both Spanish and Quechua.

All Peruvian children learn and study in Spanish at school, but in some towns where Spanish is not the main language, the townspeople have demanded that the children be taught in the local language as well. There have been cases where teachers sent by the government have been run out of the town because they were not able to teach in the local language!

Peruvians can tell which region a person comes from by the way they speak Spanish. People from Ayacucho have a soft, almost whispery way of speaking, while people from the jungle speak in a more joyful, singsong fashion.

Even though Spanish has the same alphabet as English, many letters are pronounced differently. Spanish writing uses accents and a letter that looks like English 'n', only with a moustache on top: 'ñ' (pronounced like the 'ny' in 'canyon').

SOME SPANISH WORDS AND PHRASES:
hola (oh-la) – hello
adios (a-dee-ohs) – goodbye
gracias (grah-see-ahs) – thank you
¿Cómo te llamas? (*coh*-moh tay ya-mas) –
   What is your name?

SOME QUECHUA WORDS AND PHRASES:
allinllachu (ah-yeen-*ya*-chue) – hello
qayakama (ha-ya-*kah*-mah) – goodbye
pakrasunki (pock-rah-*soon*-key) – thank you
Imataq sutiki? (ee-*mah*-tock sue-*tee*-key) –
   What is your name?

THE SPANISH AND QUECHUA WORDS IN THE BOOK

el almuerzo – lunch

Ayacuchanos – the name of the people who live in Ayacucho

Buenas noches, Ximena – Good night, Ximena

café con leche – milky coffee

el campo – the countryside

caseritas – street traders

cebiche – fish cooked with lemon

chapla – a flat bread made out of flour, water and yeast

chicha morada – a sweet drink made from purple corn

chicharrones – fried pieces of pork

chifa – Chinese food

cuy – guinea pig, a delicacy in Peru. Fried guinea pig is called *cuy frito*

escuela – school

futbolín – table football

gol – goal

Inca Kola – Peru's national soft drink

kiosko – tuck shop

llikllita – shawl

mami – mum

María Auxiliadora – Mary, Helper of Christians, the patron saint of Enrique's school

el mercado – the market

Milo – a chocolate powder that you can stir into hot milk to make a delicious drink

Pacha Mama – Mother Earth

papi – dad

Plaza de Armas – town square

polleras – the skirts worn by the Quechua women of Ayacucho

Quechua – the South American Indian people who live in the Andes mountains. Quechua is also the name of the language they speak

refrigerio – snack break or snack

Sucre – the military general who led the Battle of Ayacucho in 1824. Sucre's victory meant that Peru and South America were freed from Spanish rule

INDEX